Food for You

by Erin Duffy

 HOUGHTON MIFFLIN HARCOURT
School Publishers

PHOTOGRAPHY CREDITS: Cover © Rosenfeld/Corbis; 1 © Corbis; 2 © Rosenfeld/Corbis;
3 Nick Daly/Getty Images/Photonica; 4 © Michael Boys/Corbis; 5 © PhotoDisc; 6 © Kevin Fleming/Corbis;
7 © Jim West/Alamy; 8 © Jim West/Alamy; 9 © Somos Images/Corbis; 10 © Corbis

Printed in China

ISBN-13: 978-0-547-02840-8
ISBN-10: 0-547-02840-7

4 5 6 7 8 0940 18 17 16 15 14 13 12 11 10

Look at all the food
on the table.
How does the food get
to your table?

Some people grow fruits and vegetables in a garden at home. First they plant seeds under the ground. Then they water the seeds. Seeds need water and sunlight to grow.

The plants grow bigger
and bigger.
Soon the fruits and vegetables
are ripe.
They can go right from the
garden to the table.

Some people grow food
on small farms.
Many farms have fields for
wheat or vegetables.
Many farms have fruit trees.
Some farms have animals like
chickens and cows.

Farmers do a lot of work.
They take care of the plants
and animals.
They water the crops so they
can grow.
They feed the animals so they
can grow, too.

Farmers pick the crops.
They milk the cows and get
eggs from the chickens.
Sometimes farmers sell their
food at a market.
People love to buy these
fresh foods.

Farms can be big or small.
Some big farms have large crops
and lots of animals.
On big farms, many people pick
crops and take care of animals.

Trucks or trains take the food
to cities and towns.
You can buy the food
at the store.

Food comes from many places.
Food can come from a garden
or a farm.
Many people buy food
at a store.
Do you know where your food
comes from?

Responding

✔ **TARGET SKILL** **Author's Purpose**

Why did the author write this story? What three details tell you this? Make a chart.

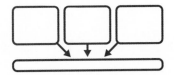

✏ Talk About It

Text to World Think of your favorite fruit or vegetable to eat. Where does it come from?

✔ **TARGET SKILL** Author's Purpose

Tell why an author writes a book.

✔ **TARGET STRATEGY** Summarize

Stop to tell important ideas as you read.

GENRE Informational text gives facts about a topic.